SPY UNIVERSITY

The Spy's Guide to Hiding Places

BY **Jim Wiese** WITH **H. Keith Melton**
SPY EXPERT

SCHOLASTIC INC.

NEW YORK   TORONTO   LONDON   AUCKLAND   SYDNEY
MEXICO CITY   NEW DELHI   HONG KONG   BUENOS AIRES

A key with a message hidden inside.

ISBN 0-439-33643-0

Copyright © 2003 by Scholastic Inc.

Editor: Andrea Menotti
Designers: Robert Rath, Lee Kaplan, Marguerite Oerlemans
Illustrations: Daniel Aycock
Photos: www.spyimages.net

12 11 10 9 8 7 6 5   4 5 6 7 8/0

Printed in the U.S.A.

First Scholastic printing, January 2003

The publisher has made every effort to ensure that the activities in this book are safe when done as instructed. Children are encouraged to do their spy activities with willing friends and family members and to respect others' right to privacy. Adults should provide guidance and supervision whenever the activity requires.

TABLE OF Contents

CC This means you'll use your Spy Gear in this activity.

CC This means you can find a related activity on the Spy University web site.

OUT

Since you started your training at Spy University, you've been collecting an impressive supply of Spy Gear. Maybe you've already thought of keeping it hidden between missions? Good idea! So, where's your hiding place?

Shhh! That's a trick question! You're not supposed to tell anyone!

A hiding place only works as long as it remains a secret, and if you have a really good spot, keep on using it. But if you haven't stashed your stuff yet, or if you've tucked it under your mattress (one of the first places someone might look), we'll show you some top-notch hiding places that are so clever, even the nosiest snoopers will be baffled!

In the spy world, even a coin can be a hiding place! This is a 10 lira coin from Italy.

As a spy trainee, you'll need to hide a lot more than just your Spy Gear. You'll also need to hide papers with top secret information, your spy notebook, and any other important materials that are for your eyes only. That's why this month's guide is dedicated to all sorts of hiding places. Wait till you see how crafty spies can be when it comes to keeping their stuff out of sight! Would you ever imagine that a working battery could have a hollow compartment for storing film, or that a coin could hold a secret message inside? Well, read on and you'll never look at batteries, coins, or even your math homework (see page 42) the same way again! But before you become a pro at *hiding*, you need to *seek* a little background knowledge to get ready for your latest round of operations.

WHY DO SPIES USE HIDING PLACES?

Spies use hiding places for three reasons:

■ **To store things.** Spies can't leave evidence of their work lying around. If someone found a spy camera or a coded message inside a spy's home, it could mean big trouble. Not only could an operation be exposed, but an entire spy career could be on the line!

OF Sight!

- **To transport things.** Spies are often on the go! To keep their tools, instructions, and other secrets safe while they're out on an operation, on the way to a meeting, or traveling, they rely on all sorts of portable hiding places.

- **To exchange things.** A big part of a spy's job is getting information, instructions, and other materials to and from a **handler**. That means spies need special hiding places where they can drop off and pick up items without arousing suspicion. The official spy term for a hiding place where materials are exchanged is a **dead drop**.

WHAT ARE THE SPECIAL TYPES OF HIDING PLACES THAT SPIES USE?

Spies sometimes hide things in rooms just like you might, by tucking them under or behind furniture, cabinets, or other fixtures. But when spies need *really* sly hiding places, they'll reach into their bag of tricks and pull out the craftiest hiding place of all: a **concealment**. A concealment is an ordinary-looking object (like a hairbrush) with a secret compartment (called a **cavity**) that can store messages, film, gadgets, or other items for spy operations. The cavity can be large enough to hold several pieces of equipment, or it can be so small that it only fits a tiny piece of film.

A clothes brush concealment.

Whether it's big or small, the beauty of a concealment is that it doesn't raise much curiosity. Since it looks like a regular, everyday object, people don't give it a second thought. Even if the wrong person picked it up, its secret would still be protected inside. When was the last time you paid really close attention to an old hairbrush (especially someone *else's* old hairbrush!)?

WHAT KINDS OF OBJECTS CAN BE USED AS CONCEALMENTS?

You name it! Almost anything can be turned into a concealment. The rule of thumb is to make sure the concealment looks as normal as possible so it doesn't attract attention. Here are some examples:

FILM HIDDEN INSIDE

- **A can of coffee with a false bottom that unscrews to reveal a storage space. (And there's still coffee in the top part!)**

- **A volleyball that opens up to hold papers inside.**

- **A false tooth with a *cavity* for small secrets.**

- **An artificial eye that can keep a tiny message out of view.**

HOW CAN SPIES KEEP THEIR HIDING PLACES SAFE?

Here are a few good rules to remember that can reduce the chances of someone finding your hiding place:

- **Leave it alone.** If you keep going back to your hiding place to make sure your stuff is there after you've hidden it, someone might see you and get curious.

- **Be normal.** Even if you have a great concealment, it wouldn't make sense to carry a can of coffee around with you at soccer practice, right? So make sure the concealment isn't only convincing, but something that won't seem out of place.

- **Don't put all your eggs in one basket.** By using several different places to hide things, you won't lose *everything* if someone discovers one of your secret spots.

- **Keep it quiet.** Don't tell anyone who's not in your **spy network** about your hiding places, even if they say they won't tell anyone else. You can never *untell* a secret once it's out!

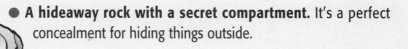

ABOUT THIS MONTH'S SPY GEAR

Ready for some hide-and-seek? Well then, you're IT! And you've got some great new Spy Gear to help you with your hiding and finding. This month, you've been issued:

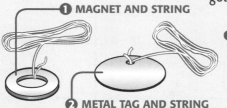

TOP VIEW

BOTTOM VIEW
DOOR TO HIDDEN COMPARTMENT

● **A hideaway rock with a secret compartment.** It's a perfect concealment for hiding things outside.

● **A secret message card, a wipe-off pen, and a deck of cards.** The secret message card looks like an ordinary playing card, but peel back the top layer, and you can write underneath with the wipe-off pen. Hide the secret message card in your deck, and you've got a great concealment!

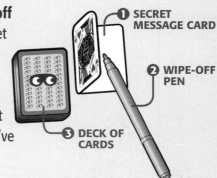

❶ **SECRET MESSAGE CARD**

❷ **WIPE-OFF PEN**

❸ **DECK OF CARDS**

❶ **MAGNET AND STRING**

❷ **METAL TAG AND STRING**

● **A magnet, a metal tag, and some string,** which will help you hide things in hard-to-reach places. See page 36 to find out more about this!

ABOUT THIS MONTH'S WEB SITE

Another on-line training session awaits you on the Spy University web site! You'll be able to test your knowledge of hiding places by searching rooms and outdoor scenes for hidden secrets. You can also take a hiding-places quiz and print out a hidden message in math code (see page 42 for more on this!). So, hop on over to **www.scholastic.com/spy** and see what you can find!

the **password** spot

This month's web site password:
hideaway

A word to wise spies

▼ Sometimes (we'll tell you when) you'll need to ask a senior spy (an adult) to help with your spy mission.

▼ Always get permission before searching for hiding places in somebody's room. Remember that people (including you!) have a right to privacy, which you should respect throughout your spy training.

▼ Never hide things in dangerous places. Avoid spots that are near poisons, electrical devices, or power outlets, and definitely stay away from places where your hidden things might catch fire (yikes!). Wise spies know that safety comes first!

SPY TALK

▼ **Cache:** A secure place to hide things. (Pronounced "cash.")

▼ **Camouflage:** To disguise something by making it blend with its surroundings.

▼ **Cavity:** The hiding space inside a concealment.

▼ **Cipher:** A form of code in which the letters of a message are replaced with a new set of letters or numbers according to some rule.

▼ **Code:** A system designed to hide the meaning of a message by substituting letters, numbers, words, symbols, sounds, or signals in place of the actual text.

▼ **Concealment:** An object that has been altered for the secret storage of messages, film, ciphers, or other items.

▼ **Counterintelligence:** The protection of information, people, and equipment from spies.

▼ **Counterspy:** Someone who works in counterintelligence, investigating and catching spies.

▼ **Dead drop:** A secret hiding place used for communication and exchange of materials between a spy and a handler.

▼ **Decoy:** Something used to fool, lure, or draw attention toward one thing and away from another.

▼ **Defect:** To leave the control of a country or intelligence service to serve another country.

▼ **Double agent:** An agent who is recruited by another country's intelligence agency to work secretly against his original agency.

▼ **Espionage:** The field of spying.

▼ **Handler:** The intelligence officer who manages an agent and gives him assignments.

▼ **Landmark:** An obvious object or place used as a reference to help you find something you've hidden.

▼ **Microdot:** A tiny photograph of a message, secret document, or other image that can only be read with a special magnifier.

▼ **Mole:** An employee of an intelligence service who secretly works for another country's intelligence service.

▼ **Spy network:** A group of spies who work together toward a common goal.

▼ **Surveillance:** The careful study of someone or something.

▼ **Systematic search:** A search that's done in a careful and orderly way, so that nothing is missed.

▼ **Tradecraft:** The set of techniques and procedures spies use to do their work.

▼ **Vault:** Any concealment or hidden compartment used to store valuables safely.

THE Hunt FOR THE SpyTREASURE

It's always sad when a favorite relative moves far away, but it's even worse when it's your fun-loving, practical-joking, all-around-awesome older brother. The house sure has been quiet since Alex left for college a few months ago.

And you weren't the only one who was sad to see Alex go—everyone in your spy network used to like learning stuff from him. He knew a lot about spying, especially when it came to hiding things. He taught you a lot (and he shared a lot of his cool spy equipment, too).

You're thinking about all of this as you're walking up to your house one day after school. As you pass the hedge, you remember how your brother used to hide a concealment rock there with messages for his friends. Just for old time's sake, you take a peek under the hedge.

And to your surprise, the rock is there!

You quickly reach down, pick up the rock, and slide open its secret compartment. There's a note inside, and it has *your* name on it!

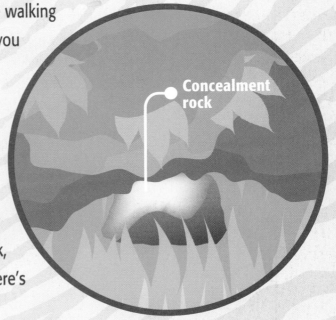

Concealment rock

You unfold the weathered paper and read:

Hey spyster!

Good job finding this note! I knew you would. Anyway, here's a challenge for you. I know you've had your eye on my spy camera for a long time. Well, guess what —it's yours, but only if you can find it! I've hidden it somewhere around the house. But before you go tearing the place apart, I've left some clues to point you in the right direction. They're written on paper just like this, and they're hidden in places where we used to hang out together. So, have a look around and see what you can find!

Your bro,
Alex

P.S. Be sure to give yourself some time!
P.P.S. Don't even *think* about calling me for hints!

Wow! Your brother's spy camera, with its awesome zoom lens! It's true—you *have* always wished it could be yours. And now it *can* be...but how are you going to find it? Alex says he's hidden clues in places where you used to hang out together, and three places come to mind right away.

The first would have to be Alex's room, where you'd go to visit him, talk, play cards, listen to music, and that kind of thing. The second would be the backyard, where the two of you would play Frisbee with your dog, Ringo. Alex was always hiding stuff there. The third place would have to be your family room, where you used to watch TV and play video games together. Alex spent a lot of time there, too, that's for sure.

But where are you going to start?

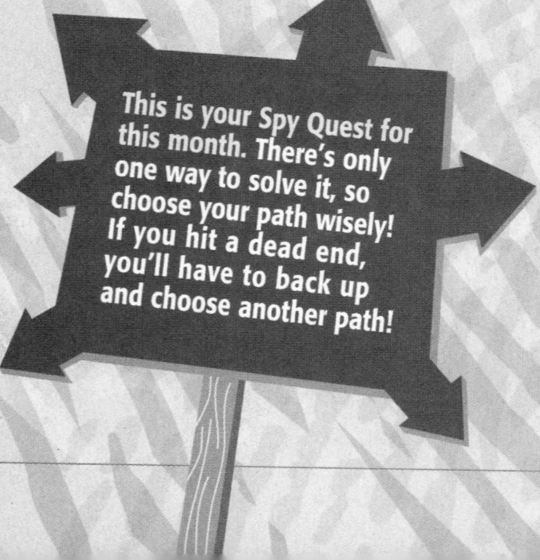

This is your Spy Quest for this month. There's only one way to solve it, so choose your path wisely! If you hit a dead end, you'll have to back up and choose another path!

■ If you decide to start looking in Alex's room, turn to **page 41**.

■ If you decide to check the backyard first, turn to **page 19**.

■ If you decide to look around the family room, turn to **page 13**.

OPERATION Rock SOLID

S o, what did you think when you first saw a rock in your Spy Gear kit? Did you think that maybe there was a mix-up in the mail, and that somewhere a rock collector was puzzling over your real spy gadget? Or did you realize right away that it wasn't a genuine chunk of stone? Well, even if you could tell by the look and feel of the rock that it wasn't real, what if you saw it buried in a garden? Would you suspect it then? Probably not!

When it comes to everyday objects, there's nothing less suspicious than an ordinary rock, and that's why it makes a great **concealment**. The **cavity** in your hideaway rock is an ideal spot for storing messages, secret information (like the lists of the **code** and **cipher** systems you use), or even small objects like a key. Rocks make great concealments for **dead drops** (when exchanging information with a **handler**), since rocks can be placed outside in well-traveled areas without attracting attention.

So, grab your hideaway rock and let's see what you can hide!

A rock concealment with papers inside. It was created by the CIA and left in a Moscow dead drop in 1977.

STUFF YOU'LL NEED

- ◎◎ Hideaway rock
- Pencil and paper
- Natural materials (other rocks, branches, seashells, pinecones)

YOUR NETWORK

- Friends to look for your hideaway rock

SPYmissions

WHAT YOU DO

PART 1: ROCK ON!

In this part of the operation, you'll practice using your hideaway rock as a dead drop to transfer information to someone else.

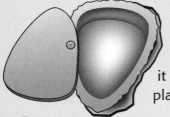

1 Open the secret compartment of your hideaway rock by turning it over and sliding the plastic bottom to the side.

2 Write a message that you want to secretly send to a friend.

3 Place the message inside the rock and close it by sliding the compartment shut.

4 Find a place to hide your rock concealment where it won't draw anyone's attention, like in a garden near other rocks. You might want to partially bury it so it looks like it's been there for a while.

Hideaway rock

5 After you've hidden your rock concealment, have a friend try to find it. Tell your friend the general area where the rock is hidden. How easy was it for your friend to find the rock? Can you think of another place to put it?

6 Try this activity again, only this time have your friend hide the rock and *you* try to find it.

PART 2: SECRET ROCK GARDEN

Your hideaway rock is also a good place to store something indoors—*if* you take the right steps to make sure it doesn't look out of place.

1 Write a message to place inside your hideaway rock. For example, you could write the code names of the members of your **spy network**, or the keys to the code and cipher systems you use.

2 Look around your room for a place where you can build a nature display of interesting things that you've found outside. Use your hideaway rock to start your display.

3 Go outside and collect things to add to your display, like different types of rocks, pieces of wood, seashells, pinecones, tree branches, and leaves.

Hideaway rock

4 Add the other items to your bedroom display, and then have another friend try to figure out your secret hiding place. Was it easy? If so, try adding more decorations around the rock to make it blend in better with its surroundings.

MORE FROM HEADQUARTERS

1 To keep messages secret even if enemy spies discover your rock concealment, you can write your notes in invisible ink. You learned how to use one kind of invisible ink, lemon juice, in your *Trainee Handbook*. Look back at your handbook if you need a refresher on that technique.

2 Another way of keeping your secret message safe is to write it in code or cipher before you hide it. Try using the Caesar cipher, which you learned in your *Trainee Handbook*.

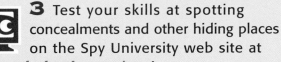 **3** Test your skills at spotting concealments and other hiding places on the Spy University web site at **www.scholastic.com/spy**!

WHAT'S THE SECRET?

While your hideaway rock is a great conceal-ment for outdoor use, you can also use it inside, if you set up the right **camouflage**, or disguise, as you learned in Part 2. By creating a display of natural items, you helped your rock blend into

This ring was created by the KGB (the intelligence service of the former Soviet Union) to conceal microdots.

its surroundings. That way, hopefully, it didn't arouse suspicion.

The cavity inside your hideaway rock might seem small, but spies work with even smaller concealments than that! One trick spies use is to shrink a big message, drawing, or map into a **microdot**. A microdot is a tiny photograph that's easy to hide and can only be read with a special magnifier.

(continued from page 10)

You head over to the family room and wonder where to start looking. There are pictures on the walls, a couple of bookcases, a sofa, a chair, and a computer desk. Since your brother always seemed to be on the computer, you decide to look there first. You find a lot of papers and disks in the desk drawers, but there's no clue for you (and no camera). The sofa and chair have nothing worthwhile in them, either, unless you count the seventy-six cents you found underneath the cushions!

After you're done with the obvious places, you decide to turn to the tougher ones. There's a wall of bookcases filled with your family's monstrous collection of books, and there's the entertainment center, which holds the TV and other electronic equipment. Which one will you tackle?

- If you decide to look in the bookcases, turn to **page 22**.
- If you decide to check the entertainment center, turn to **page 25**.

OPERATION
#2 WILDCARD

Your hideaway rock is great for hiding things in your yard or your bedroom, but what if you needed to take a secret message with you on the go? You wouldn't want to carry a rock in your pocket, would you? Ouch! That's why your Spy Gear kit includes a more portable **concealment**— a secret message card. Disguised as an ordinary playing card, the secret message card has a hidden flap that you can peel back to reveal a secret message area. The card can easily be slipped into your matching Spy Gear deck, hidden inside a book, or even carried around in your wallet. Good luck to any snooper who tries to get in on *this* game!

STUFF YOU'LL NEED

- 👓 **Secret message card**
- 👓 **Wipe-off pen**
- 👓 **Deck of cards**
- **Rubber band**
- **Tissue**

YOUR NETWORK

- **A friend to exchange secret messages with you**

WHAT YOU DO

1 The secret message card is the jack of hearts on the bottom of your Spy Gear deck. Find it, and open it by gently pulling the card's top flap away from the rest of the card. This takes a little practice. Try not to put too much pressure on the card, or you might damage the secret flap. That would make it look unusual and suspicious— not a good thing for a concealment that you're trusting with your secrets!

2 Use your wipe-off pen to write a secret note on the message area inside the card.

3 Carefully seal the flap over the message area. Your message is now safe in its hiding place.

The password is "Ace"

4 To make sure your secret message card looks innocent, place it in the middle of your deck of cards. Since your deck also has a normal jack of hearts, you'll need to remove the normal jack and set it aside.

14

5 Wrap a rubber band around the deck and pass it to your friend. Make sure your friend knows that the card with the secret message is the jack of hearts. To read your message, your friend will simply peel open the card.

6 To write a different message, open the card and use a tissue to wipe off the old message. Then write your new message using the wipe-off pen.

MORE FROM HEADQUARTERS

Turn to page 16 to learn a great spy card game you can play with your new Spy Gear deck!

WHAT'S THE SECRET?

An altered playing card is just one of the clever concealments a spy can use to hide information. If you can find or create a **cavity** in an object, then it can be used as a concealment. In this case, the key is that no one would expect a playing card to have a sneaky peel-back surface!

(continued from page 41)

You decide to search around your brother's bed. You pull off the quilt, the blanket, the sheets, and finally the mattress pad...but you find nothing. You take off the pillowcases, but there's nothing inside them (except pillows!). You check between the mattress and the box spring, and you shine a flashlight under the bed. Nothing. You even pull the bed away from the wall to check if something's hidden there.

Nothing!

If you weren't tired out before, you're *definitely* tired out now!

■ Sorry. This was a dead end. Take a quick nap if you want, then go back and try again—but only *after* you've made the bed!

During World War II (1939–1945), the British developed playing cards like your secret message card to help prisoners of war escape from behind enemy lines. When the playing cards were soaked in water, the top layer of the cards could be peeled off to reveal parts of a map. When the cards were put together in order (according to the numbers printed in the centers), they revealed a master map that could be used for planning an escape.

LOSE the MOLE!

A CARD GAME FOR SPIES

Here's a fun spy game you can play with your Spy Gear deck. It's called "Lose the Mole," and you can play it with three to seven people. First, remove the ace of clubs from your deck and set it aside. Then deal the rest of the cards to the other players. Each person should check his hand for pairs of the same color and number. So, for example, the three of diamonds could pair with the three of hearts. The players should remove the pairs and put them in a pile on the table in front of them. The pairs represent spies you

know you can trust. However, there's one card that's a **mole**—a traitorous card that secretly works for an enemy deck! The mole is the ace of spades (the card that has no pair, since you removed the ace of clubs). If you're dealt the ace of spades, unlucky you! You're starting the game with the mole in your hand! But don't worry—you'll have plenty of opportunity to get rid of the mole by passing it off to another player.

So, to begin, the players should fan their cards out and hold them with their backs facing the other players. Then someone goes first—like you, for example. You choose a card from the hand of the player to your left. You check your hand to see if the card you chose pairs up with any of the cards in your hand. If you have a pair, you take the matching card out of your hand and add

The mole.

the new pair to your pile on the table. If the new card doesn't match any of your cards, then add it to your hand.

Now the player on your left gets to choose a card from the player on his left, and the play continues around the table. The goal is to make as many pairs as you can and to finish with no cards—by *not* getting stuck with the mole! As soon as you run out of cards in your hand, you're out of the game. You're safe! The person who ends up with the mole, though, is the loser!

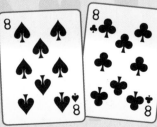

Pairs of the same number and color.

3

OPERATION
LIKE A ROCK

While looking for outdoor spots to stash your Spy Gear hideaway rock, your spy sense might have told you that rocks actually come in many sizes, shapes, and colors. Rocks can look quite different from place to place, depending on the region and the climate. Although your hideaway rock is a pretty convincing stone, there may be times when it doesn't look quite right next to other rocks around your hiding place. That's no good, since **concealments** have to look as normal and ordinary as possible. In this operation, you're going to make a rock concealment that fits right in with the rocks in your area. So, get ready to join forces with Mother Nature!

STUFF YOU'LL NEED

- Sample rock (about the size of your fist)
- Newspaper
- Measuring cup
- White glue ($1/2$ cup [125 ml])
- Empty plastic bowl (clean and dry)
- Water ($1/2$ cup [125 ml])
- Craft stick (to stir glue)
- Masking tape
- Film canister (empty)
- Ruler
- Tempera paint in the colors of your sample rock
- Paintbrush
- Plastic plate
- Dirt, moss, leaves, gravel, and other natural materials

WHAT YOU DO

1 Go outside and search for a rock around your yard or neighborhood. If you live in a city, look in a nearby park. The rock you choose should be roughly the size of your fist.

2 Examine your real rock carefully. Since you're going to use it as a model, take note of its shape, texture, and color.

3 Now it's time to get crafty! You're going to use papier-mâché (glue and paper) to make a rock just like the one you found. But *before* you start, spread newspaper over your work area to make it easier to clean up after you're done.

4 Pour about ½ cup (125 ml) of white glue into the plastic bowl. Add ½ cup (125 ml) of water to the glue and stir with a stick.

5 Make three small loops of masking tape (sticky-side out). Put one loop on the bottom of the film canister and put the other two loops on the sides of the canister.

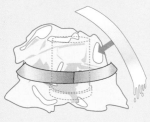

6 Take one piece of newspaper and wrap it into a ball around the film canister. The lid of the canister should face down and be even with the outer edge of the paper ball. The wad of paper should be about the same size and shape as your real rock.

Canister

7 Wrap a piece of masking tape around the newspaper wad to hold it in place. Also, tape down any edges of the newspaper that stick out.

8 Cut several sheets of newspaper into strips that are about 1 inch (2.5 cm) wide and 6 inches (15 cm) long.

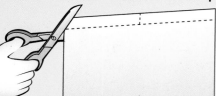

9 Hold the ends of a newspaper strip and dip one side into the glue solution. Then smooth the glue over the rest of that side of the strip with your fingers. One side of the strip should now be entirely coated in glue.

10 Starting with one end of the gluey newspaper strip, paste it onto the newspaper wad. Be careful not to cover the opening of the film canister.

11 Smooth the newspaper strip over the newspaper wad. Make sure the edges of the strip lie flat, or they'll be harder to disguise later when you paint your rock.

12 Keep adding more glue-coated newspaper strips onto the wad until it's completely covered (except for the mouth of the film canister). You'll want to have about four to six layers of newspaper around your rock. As you add the newspaper strips, keep them lumpy or smooth, depending on the shape and texture of your real rock. You can also squish the wad in some places to put bumps or dents in it. If you're having a hard time pasting the strips around the curves in the rock, try making the strips shorter or narrower.

13 When you're done, set your papier-mâché rock aside until it dries, which will probably be at least twenty-four hours later.

14 Once your rock concealment is dry, make sure that you can remove the cap from the film canister. You may need to gently peel away extra paper from around the cap to make it easier to remove.

15 Use tempera paint to color the papier-mâché rock like your sample rock. You will probably need to use several different colors and painting techniques (brush strokes, drips, and so on) to get the right look. Use the plastic plate to mix paint colors.

Would you believe that spies could conceal a secret message inside a bolt? Russian spies working in West Germany in the early 1960s did exactly that. From the outside, the bolt looked normal, but the head of the bolt could be unscrewed to reveal a hollow cavity where a rolled-up message could be hidden. Once a message was inside the bolt, the head was screwed back on, and the bolt was placed on a wooden railing on a bridge, hidden among the other bolts that held the railing together. The message was now ready to be picked up!

A hollow bolt with a rolled-up message inside.

MESSAGE

16 Paint the cap of the film canister so it blends in with the rest of your rock.

17 Now **camouflage** your rock by adding dirt, moss, leaves, gravel, and other natural materials to the surface. You can do this by putting glue on the rock, letting it dry a little, and then sticking the natural materials to the rock.

18 To hide something inside your homemade rock, just take the cap off the film canister, place the item inside the canister, and put the cap back on.

MORE FROM HEADQUARTERS

Put a message to a friend inside your homemade rock and stash it in a hiding place outside. Show your friend the general area where you've hidden the message, and see if she can discover it!

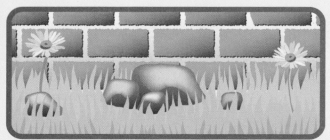

Can you spot the concealment? (Hopefully not!)

WHAT'S THE SECRET?

By making your own rock concealment to match the rocks in your area, you created a hiding place that blends in well with its environment. That's the idea here: to create something that won't attract suspicion, even if it's in plain view.

SPYquest

(continued from page 10)

You slowly circle the yard, looking for another rock concealment or anything that seems out of place. But all the rocks you pick up are the real thing. You even pick up the garden gnome that your mother insisted on putting in one of the flowerbeds, but you find nothing (except bugs) underneath.

After you search for a while longer and find nothing in the yard, you decide there are two possibilities left. Your brother could have hidden a clue in some kind of container underground, since he used to bury stuff all the time around the bushes in the back of the yard. The second place you still want to check out is the garden shed. There are many spots where stuff could be hidden in there.

- If you decide to go digging for buried treasure, turn to **page 30**.
- If you decide to investigate the garden shed, turn to **page 35**.

BOOK Smart

#4

L ots of secrets can be tucked inside a good book—and we're not talking about the kind you'll find printed *on* the pages. We're talking about the kind you can find *inside* the pages when you carve out a little compartment inside the book. This kind of **vault** might take a while to create (so be patient!), but it's definitely worth the time!

STUFF YOU'LL NEED

- An old hardcover book (see Part 1 below for the best kind)
- Ruler
- Pencil
- Scissors (with pointed ends)
- Small binder clips (optional)

YOUR NETWORK

- A senior spy to help you select the book

WHAT YOU DO

PART 1: CHOOSE THE BOOK

1 Not ready to cut up your favorite spy thriller? Well then, your first task is to find an old book that no one needs anymore. Make sure it's the kind of book that you'd be likely to have on your shelf (so no cookbooks if you're not a big chef!). It's best if the book is hardcover, because that'll make your compartment hold together better. As for size, it's up to you. The larger the book, the larger the **cavity** you'll have to

Reptiles from A to Z

2 inches (5 cm)

10 inches (25 cm)

8 inches (20 cm)

hide things. (But larger cavities require more cutting, and that means more work!) An ideal book would be about 10 inches (25 cm) long, 8 inches (20 cm) wide, and at least 2 inches (5 cm) thick.

2 Make sure you ask a senior spy to approve your choice before you get scissor-happy! *You* might think a book isn't worth saving, but someone else might treasure it!

PART 2: THE LONG CUT

1 Open the book to its twentieth page and draw a rectangle in the center, about $1\frac{1}{2}$ inches (4 cm)

from each edge. You can make a smaller rectangle if you want, but no bigger.

2 Poke one point of the scissors through the center of the rectangle to make a hole, then cut along the rectangular line.

3 Remove the rectangle you just cut out. The page should now look like a picture frame.

4 Use the pencil to outline the opening from the first cut-out page onto the page below it. To keep the page flat while you're tracing, hold the cover of the book (and all the previous pages) straight up.

5 Turn the page you already cut (the twentieth page) and start cutting out the rectangle from the page below it. Cut just outside the lines you traced, so the pencil marks get cut off along with the rest of the window.

6 Continue this process until you've cut out enough pages (probably at least a hundred) to

Binder clips

make a secret compartment in the book. As you cut the pages, make sure to keep the rectangles about the same size—people will often accidentally make each rectangle smaller than the previous one, so be careful! Every so often, it's a good idea to remeasure a page (just like you measured the first page). If you want to speed the process, you can try cutting two or three pages at a time.

To do this, however, you should use small binder clips to hold the pages together. Otherwise, the pages will move around while you're trying to cut them.

7 Now fill your secret compartment with notes, Spy Gear, or whatever else you choose to hide!

Secret Codes

8 You can use your secret book compartment to hide stuff in your room by putting the book near some others, preferably on a shelf. If you chose the right type of book, it should blend in with the rest.

Book with compartment

SEA CREATURES · STRANGE BIRDS · ROCK COLLECTING · GREAT DINOSAURS · LEAPING LIZARDS · REPTILES FROM A TO Z

MORE FROM HEADQUARTERS

After all that cutting, you might not welcome the news that your book had a built-in hiding place to begin with—but it did! Have you ever noticed the gap in the spine of a hardcover book? You can use that space to hide a note or something tiny!

WHAT'S THE SECRET?

A spy often uses several **concealments** at the same time to hide different-sized things. You can use your playing card concealment for a message, your rock concealment for folded papers and small objects, and your carved-out book for larger items like a mini-camera, a motion detector, or other Spy Gear.

(continued from page 13)

You turn your attention to the wall of bookcases in the family room. There are lots of places your brother could have hidden a clue—between, behind, or inside the books on the shelves. You take a deep breath. Might as well jump in! You start on one end of the bookcases and work your way through the books, pulling them out, flipping through them, and putting them back. There are so many books that it's taking forever!

You're just about to give up when you find the *Encyclopedia of Insects*.

As you pull the book from the shelf, you can tell there's something different about it. You hear some rattling inside it. You hold the book in front of you and open the cover. It has a secret compartment cut out of the pages! You look in the compartment and find...fruit chews?

What a sneak! Your brother always tried to hide his candy from you, and you usually found it. This is one place you never discovered before. Who would have thought your brother would keep a book concealment on the family shelves! Very clever. You pop the candy into your mouth and start chewing. Mmm....

■ That's a sweet discovery, but it's still a dead end in your search for the camera. Turn back and try again!

THE TEDDY BEAR TRICK

One spy who used a great concealment was Ruth Kuczynski, code name "Sonia." In 1941, in Oxford, England, two police constables were told that a neighbor had seen the woman next door with a transmitting radio. In those days, a radio transmitter was a cause for concern. Ordinary citizens kept their eyes open for anything, especially a transmitter, that could be a sign of an enemy spy.

The police thought this was a wild-goose chase when they were met at the door by a short, plump woman with a small child by her side. She told the constables that her name was Ruth Beurton and that she lived with her husband, Len, a sergeant in the British Royal Air Force. Mrs. Beurton looked confused when she was told by the police that they were there to look for a radio transmitter. She invited the police inside, showed them a child's toy radio, and explained that this was probably what the neighbor had seen. The police apologized and left. Only later did they learn that Ruth Beurton was actually a spy for the Soviet Union (and that the neighbor had been right)!

Ruth Kuczynski Beurton started building her **spy network** shortly

Radio

after she arrived in Oxford, England, from Geneva. As she began to gather information, she arrived at a problem: How could she transmit the information from her home in Oxford to her **handlers** inside the Soviet embassy in London? She needed a radio transmitter. But she couldn't simply purchase one in England without raising suspicion. Her solution was very crafty. Over a period of several weeks, Kuczynski made numerous trips from her home to London, with her small son clutching a teddy bear. Once in London, Soviet agents would give her a package that she placed inside the hollowed-out teddy bear. On the way back home, she and her son looked like ordinary people—only they carried the parts to build a secret radio transmitter inside the boy's bear!

It took several trips, but Kuczynski soon had her secret radio transmitter in place and was able to transmit information to her Soviet handlers for years. She seemed to sense, however, that British **counterspies** were closing in on her. In 1950, she took her family to visit relatives in Germany and was never seen in England again.

OPERATION
UNDER WHERE DRAWER

When you hear the words "secret **vault**," do you think of a safe behind a big painting, or a fake panel behind a bookshelf that opens with the press of a button? Well, you've got the right idea, but a vault doesn't have to be nearly as complicated or expensive. A vault is simply any hiding place where a spy can store items (especially larger ones) over a period of time. There are many places where a crafty spy like you can create a vault right in your own room—like under your underwear! Under *where*, you ask? Read on and find out!

STUFF YOU'LL NEED

- Ruler
- Pencil
- Corrugated cardboard
- Scissors
- Glue
- Six plastic or wooden building blocks
- 10-inch (25-cm) piece of string
- Drawer liner paper (or newspaper)

YOUR NETWORK

- A senior spy to help you cut the cardboard

WHAT YOU DO

1 To begin this activity, empty out the top drawer of your dresser. Then remove the drawer from the dresser. Place it on the floor so you can work on it.

2 Measure the length and width of the bottom of the drawer with your ruler.

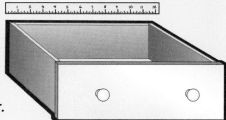

3 Use your ruler and a pencil to mark on the cardboard a rectangle that's the same size as the bottom of the drawer.

4 Using your scissors, cut out the cardboard rectangle. When you're done, the cardboard piece should fit snugly inside the drawer.

5 Next, glue one building block to each corner on one side of the cardboard. Glue the remaining two blocks along the middle of the longer edges of the cardboard. The six small plastic or wooden blocks will hold the cardboard up from the bottom of the dresser drawer. (Blocks work well because they're all the same size, but if you don't have any, you can use other items, like erasers, thread spools, or film canisters that are all the same height.)

NOTE: If you don't have six items that are the same height, you can make cardboard blocks by cutting 2 x 2-inch (5 x 5-cm) squares from corrugated cardboard. Stack the squares on top of each other as high as you want, then glue the layers together, to form a block.

6 After the glue has dried, turn the cardboard over so it's standing on the building blocks. Give it a gentle push to see if the cardboard will hold weight. If there are places where the cardboard bends easily, you may need to place more building blocks below those areas.

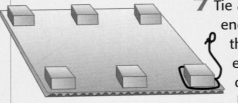

7 Tie a loop in one end of the string, then tie the other end around one of the corner blocks.

8 Place the cardboard into the bottom of the drawer so that the blocks are on the underside of the cardboard and the string loop sticks out.

9 Cover the cardboard with drawer liner paper or newspaper.

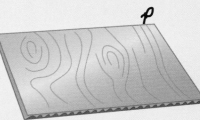

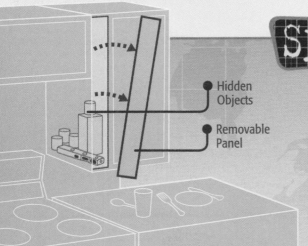

Hidden Objects

Removable Panel

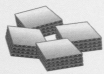

John Walker used a secret cabinet in his kitchen to conceal his spy equipment and information.

John Walker, a retired U.S. Navy warrant officer, is considered by **espionage** historians to be the most damaging spy in U.S. history. From 1967–1985, he led a ring of spies that provided so much information to the KGB (the intelligence service of the former Soviet Union) that the chairman of the KGB, Yuri Andropov (who later became the leader of the Soviet Union), referred to Walker as "Number One." It's estimated that the information provided by Walker allowed the KGB to decipher more than one million top-secret U.S. Navy messages!

Walker was eventually arrested in May 1985 and sentenced to life in prison. On the day following his arrest, a team of FBI agents searched Walker's home in Norfolk, Virginia. Walker was a "pack rat" and kept secret information and spy devices hidden throughout his house in various secret panels and holes.

If you don't have liner paper in your other drawers, you should add pieces to each drawer. That way the liner paper on the cardboard won't look suspicious.

10 To load your vault, pull the string to lift the cardboard. Place your secret things in the bottom of the drawer, making sure to leave empty spaces for the blocks to rest on the drawer bottom. Then replace the cardboard, leaving the string outside again.

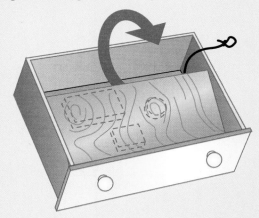

11 Put the drawer back in your dresser, and put some clothes on top of the cardboard. Your secret vault is complete!

MORE FROM HEADQUARTERS

1 If the cardboard is too flimsy to hold the weight of the clothes in your drawer, have an adult cut a piece of thin plywood the same size as the bottom of the drawer and use it instead of the cardboard. Again, cover the plywood with drawer liner paper to disguise it.

2 Look around your room for another place that could be used as a vault. Is there somewhere you could build a secret wall in your closet or on a shelf? For example, you could make a false back wall for a shelf in your closet by cutting a piece of cardboard the same size as the wall behind the shelf, then

painting the cardboard the same color as the wall. You could then use building blocks or film canisters to hold the cardboard away from the wall, similar to what you did in this operation.

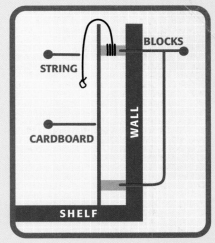

Don't forget to attach a string to one of the blocks so you can open the vault later!

WHAT'S THE SECRET?

Although a secret vault can hide more items than a rock concealment, all hiding places have limited space. That's why it's important for spies to keep only what they need, and to use lots of different hiding places! If your drawer vault is too full or if you put something too large inside, it could look obvious to a snoop!

(continued from page 13)

You head for the entertainment center and open it up, revealing a television, a VCR, and a stereo system inside. There really isn't anywhere your brother could have hidden something without damaging the equipment or going behind it where all the wires are. You know that your brother is too smart to use a hiding place that would put you in danger or get either of you into trouble!

■ The entertainment center is a dead end. Take a cartoon break, then turn back and try again.

OPERATION ENVELOPE Please

Need to hide something in a hurry? Then you've come to the right place! While making a **vault** in a book or a drawer can take a long time (as you saw in **Operation Book Smart** and **Operation Under Where Drawer**), this operation will show you how to create a handy, easy-to-access pouch in seconds! The secret? An envelope, please! That's right—you can stick an envelope that's loaded with secret papers in all kinds of clever spots. Read on to get some ideas!

STUFF YOU'LL NEED

- Envelope (letter size)
- Secret papers
- Tape

WHAT YOU DO

1 Fill an envelope with secret papers (like coded messages). Don't seal the envelope—just tuck in the flap.

2 Put a large piece of tape across the back of the envelope (below the flap), making sure that the tape sticks to the envelope and hangs over both edges so that it can be used to attach the envelope to things.

3 Look around your room. Do you see places where you could stick the envelope so that no one will find it? If you can't think of any places right away, here are a few ideas to get you started.

■ Tape the envelope to the back of a picture that's hanging on a wall in your room.

■ Tape the envelope to the inside of a book jacket. Unless the book jacket is removed, no one will know it's there.

■ Tape the envelope to the bottom of your desk, either at home or at school.

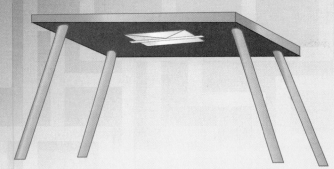

■ Tape the envelope underneath your computer's keyboard.

■ Tape the envelope to the inside of your closet wall, just above the door. No one ever looks up there!

■ Tape the envelope to the bottom (or back) of a drawer in your desk or dresser. Unless someone takes the drawer completely out, they won't find the envelope.

4 If you need the information in the envelope, just go to your hiding place, lift up the flap, and pull out the papers. You can put them back inside when you're done.

MORE FROM HEADQUARTERS

If you have a box where you save old mail and birthday cards, you can put your secret envelope in there. Disguise your envelope so it looks like the others in the box. (You might even write "With love from Grandma" on it!)

WHAT'S THE SECRET?

Envelopes have many advantages, including being cheap, disposable, and quick to load or unload. Plus, envelopes are used every day for non-spy activities, so even if people see your secret pouch, they might not get curious right away. And to keep their curiosity at bay, remember: Your secrets will be safer if you *don't* write "TOP SECRET" on the envelope!

(continued from page 44)

What? You're checking the *freezer*? Before you deep-freeze your fingers sifting through the peas and carrots, you'd better try decoding that message again!

■ This a dead end. Turn back and try again!

OPERATION BURIED TREASURE

Okay, spy trainee, by now your head should be jam-packed with lots of information on hiding places, from tiny **concealments** to great big **vaults** and everything in between. You've learned how to hide things indoors, and you've seen how hideaway rocks can be useful for **dead drop** transfers or for outdoor storage. So here's a pop quiz: What if you needed to hide something outside, but it was too big for your rock concealments? Where would you put it? Stumped? All right, here's a clue: How about looking under your feet? That's right, you can hide things in a **cache** (a secret hiding place) underground! Intrigued? Then *dig* into this next activity!

STUFF YOU'LL NEED

- **Pencil and paper**
- **Clean, empty plastic container with a lid (like a cottage cheese container, or a plastic jar with a screw-top lid)**
- **Tape**
- **Shovel**
- **Lemon juice** ⎫
- **Bowl** ⎬ optional
- **Cotton swab** ⎭

YOUR NETWORK

- **A senior spy to approve your digging location**

WHAT YOU DO

PART 1: DIG TIME

1 Write a message on a piece of paper.

2 Place the message inside the container and secure the lid. If you're going to leave the information outside for a long time, you should tape the lid to the container so that no water can enter the container and spoil the message.

3 Find a place in your yard where (with approval from your senior spy) you can bury the container. Dig a hole that's big enough so that the container will be at least 6 inches (15 cm) below ground.

4 Place the container in the hole and then fill the hole back up with dirt.

5 Spread the dirt around so that the place where you dug the hole isn't obvious.

PART 2: TREASURE MAP!

1 Using pencil and paper, draw a map of the area where you've buried the container. Include any **landmarks**, such as trees or bushes, that will help you find your cache later on.

2 A good way to hide the container's location on the map is to mark the spot using an invisible ink like lemon juice. If you don't remember how to use lemon juice for invisible ink, reread that section in your *Trainee Handbook*.

3 When you need to remember the location of your cache, just develop your invisible ink. Or, if you want to give a friend instructions on how to find your cache, you can pass your

friend the map and explain how to develop the invisible ink.

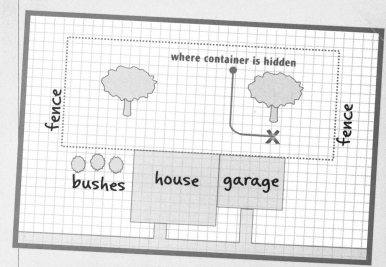

where container is hidden

fence   fence

bushes   house   garage

MORE FROM HEADQUARTERS

1 Besides burying a secret item, where else can you hide things outside? Look around your yard or the building where you live. What spots might make good hiding places? To get you started, here are a few examples of places to hide a secret message:

- Hide the message among the gardening supplies.

- Put the message under a planter on the porch.

- Camouflage the message with leaves and tie it to the branch of a tree or bush.

- Place the message beneath a doormat.

- Find a rock in the garden, lift it, and place the message beneath it. Then put the rock back exactly as you found it.

29

■ Tape or thumbtack the message beneath a lawn chair or picnic table.

 2 On the Spy University web site at **www.scholastic.com/spy**, you can scan outdoor scenes for hidden treasures! How much can you uncover before time is up? Stop by and find out!

This flowerpot has a hidden cavity for storing film. It was made for use inside an apartment, and it was opened by unscrewing the base.

CAVITY FOR STORING FILM

BASE OF FLOWERPOT

When hiding things outside, a hole in the ground or just about any small opening can be used. Remember, though, that you should always ask an adult where it's okay to dig. Be careful when digging around flowers, shrubs, and bulb plants, and never dig around pipes or wires that come out of the ground, since that could be dangerous.

SPYquest

(continued from page 19)

You grab a shovel and head over to the back of the yard, where Alex used to bury stuff. You're encouraged when you see that the ground looks like it was dug up pretty recently. After all, Alex could have set this whole thing up while he was at home a month ago—who knows.

You start digging, checking each shovel of dirt for some kind of container with a clue inside. There's no container, but there are a lot of lumpy things that look kind of like onions and some creepy-looking bugs. Gross! Soon, you have a pretty big hole. You're about to keep digging when you hear a familiar voice demand, "What do you think you're doing?!"

Turning around, you see your mom storming across the lawn, looking furious. Bending over, she picks up one of the brown lumps on top of the pile of dirt and frowns at you. "You just dug up my tulip bulbs!"

Uh-oh! You get in big trouble, and your mom makes you replant all the bulbs. As you're patting the dirt on top of the last bulb, you can hear Alex telling you, "Never dig without checking with Mom first. You never know where her latest garden project is going to be!"

■ If only you'd remembered! This is a dead end. Go back and try another path!

OPERATION
#8 Forget MeNOT

STUFF YOU'LL NEED
- **Two pieces of paper**
- **Pencil**
- **Two paper clips**

Have you ever watched a squirrel bury a nut and wondered if he'd remember where the nut was when he came looking for it later? Well, as a spy, you face the same challenge when it comes to remembering all of your hiding places. You've already learned that drawing a map can help remind you where something is buried in an underground **cache** (in **Operation Buried Treasure**). But to be safe, it's a good idea to hide the map, too! That means another hiding place! So, how do you keep all of your hiding places straight? Try this operation to see how a special map system can help you make sure you don't hide your secrets from yourself!

WHAT YOU DO

1 Choose five different places in your room where you want to hide things. For example, you may choose to hide one thing inside a book **concealment** on your desk, one in a pack of cards on your shelf, one in a box in your closet, another in an envelope taped under your rug, and the last in a **vault** in your sock drawer.

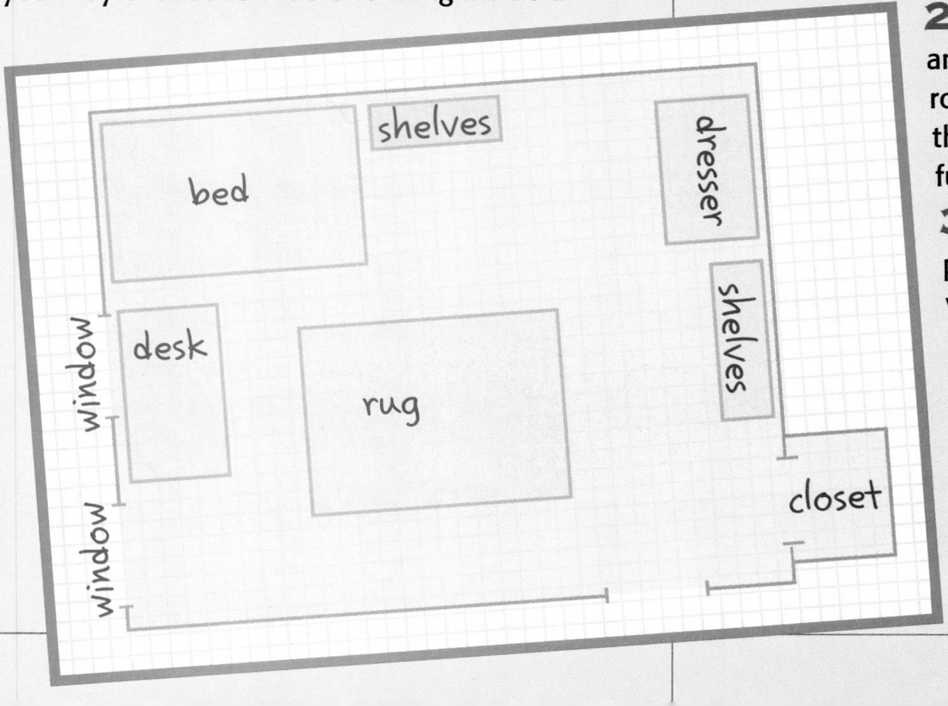

2 Take a plain piece of paper and draw a sketch of your room from above, including the doors, windows, and furniture.

3 Take a second piece of plain paper and place it over your map. Hold it in place using the paper clips.

4 Hold the two papers against a window (during the day). You should be able to see the map through the top sheet of paper.

shelves

bed

dresser

shelves

window

desk

rug

window

closet

31

5 Mark an X on the top sheet of paper above each of your five hiding places on the map below.

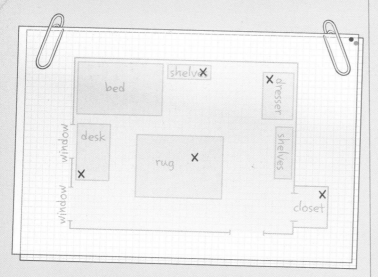

6 Make a small dot in the upper right corner of the top sheet, and do the same on the map. This way, you'll always know how to place the papers together.

7 Separate the top sheet with the X's from the bottom sheet with the map. Place each sheet in a different location in your room. That way no one will know that they're meant to go together.

8 Now, if you ever forget your hiding places, or if you want to share them with someone else, you have a two-layered treasure map! Just place the sheet with the X's underneath the sheet with the map, making sure that the dot is in the upper right corner of each sheet. Hold both sheets up to the light, and your hiding places will shine through.

MORE FROM HEADQUARTERS

Give a friend both sheets of your map, and see if she can use it to find your hiding places. How quickly can she uncover your secrets?

WHAT'S THE SECRET?

A good memory is something that comes in handy for everyone, not just spies. But just like taking notes in class or keeping to-do lists, writing down hiding places is a good backup to relying on memory alone. In this activity, you used a secret map system to keep a record of your hiding places. You might not ever need it, but it's a lot easier to take a few simple steps now than to hunt all over for your well-hidden secrets later!

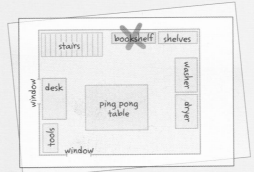

SPYquest

(continued from page 44)

You open your brother's closet in search of the ugly slipper. You're sure your brother is referring to the slippers your grandma gave him for his birthday last year—those fuzzy green ones he never wore. Sure enough, you find the slippers in the back of the closet, and you reach deep into their toes. In one of them, you find a folded piece of paper.

Excitedly, you unfold the piece of paper to reveal a sketch of a room. After scanning it for a second, you realize it's your basement! But what are you supposed to do with this?

Then you realize—that's what the sheet with the X is for! It's a treasure map in two layers! You grab the sheet with the X and place it under the map, and when you hold the two papers up to the light from the window, it's clear. The X is over the bookshelf in the basement!

■ Better head down there! Turn to **page 38**!

GRIN

and WEAR IT

When spies are on the road, the secret spy stuff they carry with them *better* be well hidden. If a spy gets stopped and searched at a border crossing, his hiding places have to hold up to a tough inspection. That's why spies have developed all kinds of clever ways to hide things on their bodies—in clothes, in shoes, and even in their *teeth* and *eyes* (turn back to page 6 if you haven't seen those hiding places yet!). In this operation, you're going to learn some quick and easy (but still very sneaky) ways to wear your secrets. Just make sure to separate your secrets from your clothes before putting them in the wash!

STUFF YOU'LL NEED

- Scissors
- Tea bag
- Safety pins
- Coat
- Paper and pencil

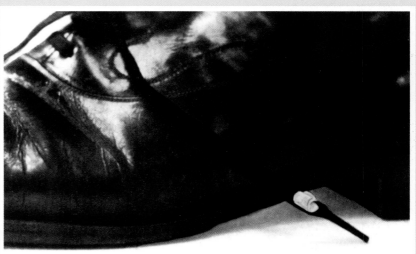

A secret message hidden in a spy's shoelace!

WHAT YOU DO

1 Cut off the top of the tea bag and pour out the tea. Now you have a small open pouch.

During World War I (1914–1918), two French spies posed as traveling saleswomen, operating **spy networks** in France, Belgium, and Holland for British intelligence. Marie-Léonie Vanhoutte, code name "Charlotte," posed as a traveling seller of cheeses, and Louise de Bettignies, code name "Alice Dubois," posed as a maker and seller of lace.

De Bettignies was an expert at **concealments** who came up with inventive ways to hide her messages so that the Germans wouldn't find them. She hid information in balls of knitting yarn and in children's toys, artificial limbs, sausages, and candy bars. She even hid a tiny map of enemy fortifications in the rim of a pair of eyeglasses!

De Bettignies was once arrested and searched for hidden messages. Chemicals were even applied to her skin in the hope that invisible writing would be revealed. Unknown to the Germans, the real secret information had been written on a piece of paper the size of a grain of rice and was hidden beneath De Bettignies's tongue!

2 Use the safety pins to attach the tea bag inside the sleeve of your coat near the cuff. The open end of the tea bag should face away from your cuff, and the tea bag should be pinned so that it can be easily reached by you, but not easily seen by others when you're wearing the coat.

3 Write a secret message on a small piece of paper. Fold the paper in half twice and place it in the pouch in your sleeve. If you're concerned that the message will fall out, you can close the pouch with masking tape or another safety pin.

4 Hang your coat in the closet. Your message is safe there, since few people would bother searching inside the sleeves of a hanging coat! If you need to take the message with you somewhere, you can just put on the coat, walk out the door, and grin as you wear your secret!

MORE FROM HEADQUARTERS

Besides a secret compartment in your coat sleeve, there are many other places on your body or in your closet where you can hide messages and other materials. Here are a few ideas to get you started:

■ Hide a message behind your belt. You can tape a tea bag pouch to the underside of your belt, or you can fold your secret papers and tape them directly onto the belt.

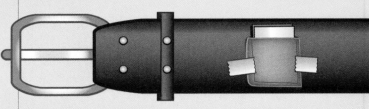

■ Hide a message inside your hatband.

■ Hide a message in your sock.

■ Place extra-secret information under the insole of your shoe. This is not always easy to get to, but it's a safe place to hide secret messages.

This shoe has a hollow heel for secret storage.

CAVITY FOR STORING FILM

WHAT'S THE SECRET?

There are lots of great places where spies can hide stuff in their clothes. The key is finding a spot where no one would think to check. What kinds of clothing concealments can you invent? Maybe the photos on this page will give you some inspiration!

A secret message can hide behind a button!

(continued from page 19)

You turn your attention to the garden shed. There are bags of potting soil, rows of empty clay pots, and several boxes that are stored on the shelves way up high. You search throughout the shed and still can't find anything that looks like a clue (or a camera for that matter!). But how about looking in the boxes on the shelves? You pull up a ladder so you can reach them.

There's nothing in the first two boxes, but the third box is heavier. Maybe that's where your brother hid the camera! You give the box a tug to pull it down, but you lose your balance and fall a couple of feet to the floor. The box lands beside you. *Thump!*

You dust yourself off, open the box and find…presents? Inside the box are colorfully wrapped gifts, each with a different family member's name on it.

You know Mom is the only one in the family who gets her gift shopping done early, so they must be hers. No wonder you can never find any gifts when you search the house in the days before the holidays!

That was a clever hiding place, and a fun find, but you're no closer to the camera.

___

■ This is a dead end. Go back and try again!

OPERATION

G○FISH!

#10

Sometimes, rather than actually hiding things away, people simply put things they don't want others to mess with out of reach. You've probably experienced a cookie jar that was kept up high on a shelf before, right? So why not combine the idea of using hard-to-reach places with some great spy technology that'll keep everyone's hands off your Spy Gear? It's a pretty *attractive* idea, as you'll see when you try out this operation!

STUFF YOU'LL NEED

- 👓 **Spy Case and other Spy Gear that needs to be hidden**
- 👓 **Metal tag on string**
- 👓 **Magnet on string**

WHAT YOU DO
PART 1:
SETTING THE BAIT

Let's put your Spy Gear into a hiding place that no one can get to.

1 Place your Spy Gear into your Spy Case and zip it up.

2 Locate a large piece of furniture that sits up against a wall and can't easily be moved (like a dresser or a bookcase). The furniture should not be made of metal!

SPACE BETWEEN WALL AND BOOKCASE

There should be enough space between the furniture and the wall to fit your Spy Case.

3 Take the string with the metal tag on one end and tie it securely around the handle of your Spy Case.

4 Use the string to lower the Spy Case behind the piece of furniture. When the Spy Case is on the floor behind the furniture, release the rest of the string and the metal tag. Your Spy Gear is now hidden from view.

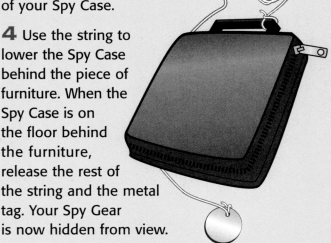

x
36

PART 2: GETTING A BITE

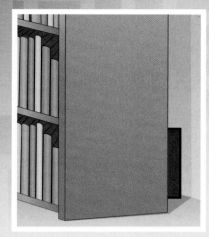

Now *go fish* and get your Spy Gear out!

1 To retrieve your Spy Gear, lower the magnet on the string behind the piece of furniture.

2 Slowly move the string back and forth until the magnet sticks to the metal tag.

3 Pull the magnet's string up until you can grab the string attached to the metal tag. Then pull that string until you can grab your Spy Case.

MORE FROM HEADQUARTERS

If you're working with a very tall piece of furniture, try tying the magnet's string to a stick or a broom handle, making what looks like a fishing pole. Hold the fishing pole and slowly move it back and forth until the magnet sticks to the metal tag. Use the pole to pull the metal tag up, then grab the string attached to the metal tag and pull your Spy Case out.

SPYtales

Ashot Akopyan, code name "Euphrates," a spy for the Soviet Union in Italy in 1955, hid the Minox camera he used for making copies of secret documents inside a wall in his apartment. By lifting the tiles in the ceiling, he was able to access some empty space within the wall. He used a magnet on the end of a fishing rod to retrieve his camera from its hiding place. His technique worked so well that the Italian **counterintelligence** service never located his equipment.

Akopyan eventually returned safely to the Soviet Union and later taught the technique to young Soviet intelligence officers learning about the craft of espionage, just as you are in Spy University!

Ashot Akopyan, Russian spy, using a magnet to retrieve a camera from a hiding place behind a wall.

WHAT'S THE SECRET?

This technique uses magnetism to retrieve hidden goods. The magnet only has to be strong enough to stick to the metal tag, so you can get a hold of the string that's attached to your gear. The magnet doesn't need to be strong enough to lift the Spy Gear itself (since *you* lift the gear when you pull the string).

Magnets can be used in other ways to help hide things. Intelligence agencies working in Soviet bloc countries (those that supported the Soviet Union during the Cold War [1945–1991]) used a special battery to hide and transfer small items. Inside the casing of a standard flashlight battery was a **cavity** in which film, money, or even **microdot** cameras and viewers could be hidden. There was also a much smaller, working battery inside. This allowed the battery to work like normal (but still have plenty of space inside to store things). To open the fake battery, the bottom had to be unscrewed using a magnet.

Battery concealments like this were often hidden inside working flashlights.

INNER BATTERY (AA SIZE)

SHELL OF LARGER BATTERY

SPYquest

(continued from page 32)

You run into the basement and find your brother's fishing pole leaning against the bookshelf. You walk over to the rod and, sure enough, you find a note on it that says, "Happy fishing."

You check out the end of the fishing line and find a magnet. You've seen this spy trick before! Your brother showed it to you once! You reel out some line, and then lower the magnet behind the bookcase. You slowly move the magnet back and forth. Then suddenly, you hear the magnet stick to something. You begin to reel in the line and soon find that the magnet is stuck to a piece of metal, and the metal piece is tied to some string. You grab the string and pull on it, and slowly a plastic bag comes up and over the top of the book-shelf. You carefully lower the plastic bag to the floor and open it. Inside the bag are a note and your brother's spy camera!

You read the note. It says:

■ Congratulations indeed!
Quest accomplished!

Way to go, spyster! You found the camera, so it's yours! Now give me a call so I can congratulate you!

#11

FINDERS
KeeperS

By now you're a pro at hiding things in lots of different places. But what if **counterspies** searched your room? Would they find your hiding places?

Possibly! That's because counterspies are equipped with special training and techniques to help them search a room thoroughly. Don't worry, we'll let you in on their secret methods—because learning how to *search* for secrets will make you even better at *hiding* them!

WHAT YOU DO
PART 1:
HIDE-AND-SEEK

For this operation, pretend that a spy has stolen some secret information and stored it on a CD, and your job is to find out where the CD is hidden in the spy's headquarters. For this exercise, your bedroom will serve as the spy's HQ!

1 Give your friend a CD to hide in your bedroom.

2 Leave the room for two minutes while your friend hides the CD.

3 After the CD has been hidden, try to find it. Give yourself ten minutes. If you have trouble, ask your friend to give you hints by saying "warmer" when you're getting closer to the CD and "colder" when you're getting farther away. If you can't find the CD before time is up, have your friend show you where it's hidden.

4 Now it's your turn. Hide the CD and let your friend try to find it. See how well your hiding place holds up to your friend's searching skills!

PART 2:
DO A DOUBLE TAKE

In Part 1, you may have found what you were looking for, but you may not have searched the room the way counterspies would. They use a **systematic search** so they don't overlook any locations.

1 Leave the room and have your friend hide the CD again.

2 When you return to the room this time, use a systematic search pattern:

- Begin by searching the room at eye level and higher.

- Start at the left of the door and move clockwise around the room until you reach the door again.

- Next, search the room from eye to waist level, again starting and finishing at the door.

- Finally, search the room from waist level to the floor.

3 Were you able to find the hiding place more quickly and easily using a systematic search?

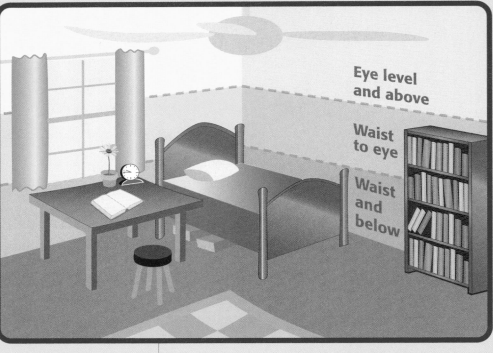

Eye level and above

Waist to eye

Waist and below

MORE FROM HEADQUARTERS

1 Have your friend hide the CD in another room, then try to find it using a systematic search. As you get better at searching, try bigger rooms!

2 Try searching a room with a team of two or more people. Each team member can search a different height as you move around the room. For example, one person can search above eye level, one between eye and waist level, and one from waist level to the floor. See how much more quickly the CD can be found with more people on the job!

SPYtales

Colonel Oleg Penkovsky was a Russian **mole** who spied for the United States and Great Britain in the early 1960s. An officer in the Soviet Union's military intelligence service (the GRU), Penkovsky passed information to the CIA and MI6 (the British foreign intelligence service) about Soviet military operations. He supplied so much information that the CIA set up a team of twenty translators and analysts to handle it, and MI6 added a dozen more. The information Penkovsky revealed was so important, it's said to have helped the world avoid a nuclear conflict between the United States and the Soviet Union in 1962. Unfortunately, however, Penkovsky was arrested by the Soviets on October 22, 1962, found guilty of spying on his country, and executed in 1963. Penkovsky's spy equipment included miniature Minox cameras and supplies, and special **codes** that were hidden in a secret compartment in his desk.

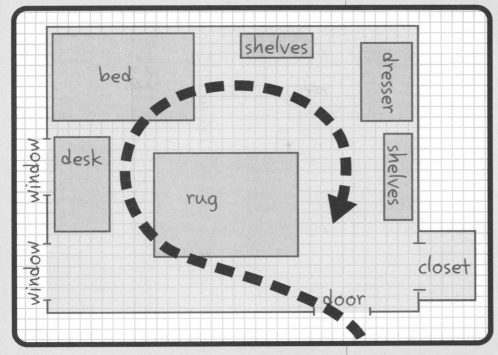

Map labels: window, window, window, bed, desk, shelves, rug, dresser, shelves, closet, door

3 Stop by the Spy University web site at **www.scholastic.com/spy** and test your systematic searching skills. See if you can find hidden secrets in a room before time runs out!

WHAT'S THE SECRET?

A systematic search is the most thorough way to look for hidden secrets. By repeating this operation several times and with several different people, you'll not only get used to the method, but you'll also become familiar with the kinds of hiding places people use most often (like under a bed, or between the mattress and box spring). So the next time you really want to hide something well, you'll know to avoid the usual spots!

A word to wise spies

Remember that you shouldn't search anyone's room without permission.

SPYquest

(continued from page 10)

You decide to do a systematic search of your brother's room. You start by the door and work your way around the room in a clockwise direction. You focus first on the area from your eye level up to the ceiling. You check behind pictures and along the shelves. After you go around the room once, you start over, this time checking the area from eye to waist level, including your brother's drawers, nightstand, and desktop. The final circle around the room is from waist level to the floor, and that's when you (finally!) find the clue. When you lift up the corner of the rug, you find a note taped to the underside! It reads:

> Guess what, spyster — you found a clue! Congrats! That's good work so far. I know searching can really tire you out, but remember — these things take time.

Is this your brother's idea of *clue*? You study the note carefully. Maybe there's a hidden clue in the message? But what could it be? The words "tire you out" could be a hint to search the bed. Or what about the phrase "these things take time?" Alex also mentioned time on his first note, you remember. Maybe your brother is directing you to a clock?

- If you decide to search your brother's bed, turn to **page 15.**

- If you decide to check out the alarm clock on your brother's nightstand, turn to **page 44.**

OPERATION
NUMBER CRUNCHER

Before we leave you this month, there's one final hiding place for you to master. How about burying a secret in your math homework? That's right—we've got a **code** that'll turn your secret messages into math problems! So, grab your pencil and paper, and let's get calculating!

WHAT YOU DO

PART 1: READING BETWEEN THE NUMBERS

1 Suppose you received the following letter from your spy network. You know that a secret message is hidden in it. But can you figure it out?

> Math homework
>
> $\begin{array}{r} 19.05 \\ + 3.18 \\ \hline \end{array}$ $\quad$ $\begin{array}{r} 5.20 \\ +13.05 \\ \hline \end{array}$ $\quad$ $\begin{array}{r} 5.20 \\ + 9.14 \\ \hline \end{array}$
>
> $\begin{array}{r} 7.01 \\ +6.20 \\ \hline \end{array}$ $\quad$ $\begin{array}{r} 5.18 \\ +19.03 \\ \hline \end{array}$ $\quad$ $\begin{array}{r} 8.15 \\ +15.12 \\ \hline \end{array}$

2 To translate the hidden message, use the pencil and paper to write down the numbers as they appear in each problem. Starting with the first problem, work left to right in the top row, then the bottom row (in this example, the first numbers so far are 19.05.3.18).

3 Move to the second problem and do the same. The numbers would now be 19.05.3.18.5.20.13.05.

4 Continue until you have all the numbers written out in a line.

5 Convert each number into a letter using the chart below.

NOTE: When a number from 1 to 9 is on the left of the decimal point, it's simply written by itself. But when a number from 1 to 9 is written to the right of the decimal, it's written with a zero in front of it.

A	B	C	D	E	F	G	H	I	J	K	L	M	N	O	P	Q	R	S	T	U	V	W	X	Y	Z
1	2	3	4	5	6	7	8	9	10	11	12	13	14	15	16	17	18	19	20	21	22	23	24	25	26

6 Break the letters into words. What does the message say? Check your answer on page 48. If you got it right, then you get an A on your math homework!

PART 2:
A QUICK STUDY

1 Think of a message you want to send to a friend. For our example, we'll write "I need your number."

2 Substitute each letter in the message with the number below it in the chart on page 42.

I	N	E	E	D		Y	O	U	R		N	U	M	B	E	R
9	14	5	5	4		25	15	21	18		14	21	13	2	5	18

3 Now turn the numbers into math problems by arranging them on the page from left to right and from top to bottom. When you get to the end of the message, you may be in the middle of a number (if your message has an odd number of letters). If this is the case, just put two zeros after the decimal point, as shown below.

$$
\begin{array}{ccc}
9.14 & 4.25 & 18.14 \\
+5.05 & +15.21 & +21.13 \\
\end{array}
$$

$$
\begin{array}{c}
2.05 \\
+18.00 \\
\end{array}
$$

4 If your message ends with a lone number without a math problem, you can make the final problem have three numbers, as shown below.

You are a spy =

$$
\begin{array}{cc}
25.15 & 18.05 \\
+21.01 & 1.19 \\
& +16.25 \\
\end{array}
$$

SPYtales

Numbers can be used to send secret messages in other ways. Dusko Popov (code name "Tricycle") was a Yugoslavian businessman who also worked as a **double agent** for both the British and Germans (who were on opposite sides during World War II [1939–1945]). But before Popov became a double agent, he spied for German military intelligence (the Abwehr) in Portugal. He learned where and when he was supposed to meet his **handlers** by visiting a casino. While he was sitting at a roulette table, another agent would place chips on numbers in the betting area. The numbers were a code that told Popov when and where his next meeting would take place. "It was an expensive code," Popov admitted later, since the chips weren't cheap, and a lot of them were gambled away during this process! By the way, if this glamorous technique sounds like something out of a James Bond movie, you're not too far off. Popov is thought to be the real-life inspiration for "007" himself!

5 Add plus (+), minus (–), or multiplication (x) signs to complete your math problems. You can even add dollar ($) signs if you want to make it look like you're calculating dollar amounts.

6 Pass the coded message to your friend. Make sure that he knows how to translate it by converting each number back to a letter, and then separating the letters into words.

MORE FROM HEADQUARTERS

1 Can you figure out this message? You can check your answer on page 48!

$$\begin{array}{cccc} 25.15 & 1.14 & 21.14 & 14.13 \\ +21.03 & +3.15 & +20.15 & +5.00 \end{array}$$

2 You can make this code harder to break by starting the numbering system at a letter other than A. For example, start numbering the alphabet below the letter E, so E is 1, F is 2, and so on.

3 On the Spy University web site (**www.scholastic.com/spy**), you can use a Math Code Machine to encode a message and make it look just like a real math worksheet! Then you can print out the worksheet and pass it on to a friend!

WHAT'S THE SECRET?

This code uses numbers to represent the letters in a message. It's actually a substitution **cipher**, because a number is substituted for each letter in the message.

SPYquest

(continued from page 41)

You check the alarm clock on your brother's nightstand, since it's the only clock in the room. You pick it up, hoping there might be a note underneath, but there's nothing. Then, as you turn the clock around, you see that there's an arrow drawn on the back in black marker, and it's pointing down. That must be a clue!

You figure the arrow must be pointing to the drawer in your brother's nightstand—but you've looked there already! Could you have missed something? You open the drawer again, and you search through the items one more time. There's a flashlight, a chewed-up pen, a couple of magazines, a key chain from Miami, and a book with a torn-off cover. You

search each of the items inside and out, just in case they're concealments. After a while, it's clear they're not.

What could you be missing? Then it hits you. Your brother told you about drawer vaults a while ago—what if this drawer has a false bottom? You check, and sure enough, you find a tiny string along the side of the drawer.

You pull the string, and the bottom of the drawer lifts to reveal a vault underneath. There are two things inside.

One is a blank piece of paper with a single X mark on it, and the other is a piece of notebook paper with math problems on it. You set aside the paper with the X for now, because you recognize that the math problems are really a message in code!

You quickly decode the message, and you smile when you see what it says. Now you know exactly where to look for your next clue!

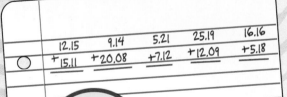

$$\begin{array}{ccccc} 12.15 & 9.14 & 5.21 & 25.19 & 16.16 \\ +15.11 & +20.08 & +7.12 & +12.09 & +5.18 \end{array}$$

Psst. You can check your answer on page 48.

X

■ If you're going to look among the shoes in your brother's closet, turn to **page 32**.

■ If you're going to check the freezer, turn to **page 27**.

The Hollow Nickel

On June 22, 1953, a newspaper delivery boy named Jimmy knocked on an apartment door in Brooklyn, New York, to collect his payment. The customer needed some change, but Jimmy didn't have enough, so he knocked on a neighbor's door to ask for change for a dollar. Two women answered the door and, after digging through their pocketbooks, gave Jimmy the change he needed. Jimmy went back to his customer, collected his payment, and went on his way.

As Jimmy walked out of the apartment building, jingling some coins in his hand, he noticed that one of the coins had a strange ring to it. It was a nickel, and when Jimmy picked it up, he could feel that it was lighter than the other nickels in his hand. As a test,

Jimmy dropped the coin to the floor. To his surprise, it split open! Inside the coin was a tiny photograph showing a series of numbers. Jimmy was amazed. This was clearly no ordinary coin! In fact, Jimmy had accidentally discovered a **concealment** made by a Russian spy. But it would take American **counterspies** years to piece together the puzzle!

Jimmy mentioned the mysterious coin to a friend, whose father was a police officer. The police officer in turn told a detective of the New York City Police Department, who asked Jimmy for the coin and then handed it over to the FBI (Federal Bureau of Investigation). When FBI experts examined the coin, they found a tiny hole drilled into its face, right in the R of the word "TRUST."

The hollow nickel, outside and inside.

The coin could be opened by sticking a fine needle into this hole.

FBI agents also carefully examined the tiny photograph (a **microdot**), which contained ten columns of numbers. Each number was five digits long, and there were twenty-one numbers in most of the columns. The FBI agents immediately suspected that this was a message in **cipher**. But key questions remained unanswered: What did the message say, and who was the spy behind all this?

The FBI interviewed the two women who had given Jimmy change for his dollar. The women remembered the boy, but they insisted that they had not given him the hollow nickel. "We've never even *seen* a hollow coin," they said. FBI agents then collected information on hollow coins and interviewed people from all over the world, including the makers of magic tricks, to try to find the person responsible for the nickel concealment. But for the next four years, all of the FBI's leads turned out to be dead ends.

Finally, in May 1957, the FBI interviewed a Russian spy named Reino Hayhanen who wanted to **defect** to the United States (so he could avoid his orders to return to Moscow). For five years, from 1952 to 1957, Hayhanen had been spying for the KGB (the intelligence service of the former Soviet Union) in New York City, living under the name of Eugene Maki. Hayhanen told the FBI that he used many concealments—hollow pens, pencils, screws, and batteries—in his exchanges with his **handler**. He also showed the FBI a coin from Finland. It had been hollowed

out, and there was a small hole in the tail side, similar to the hole in Jimmy's nickel from years before. Because of the similarity between the two coins, the FBI was now convinced that Jimmy's nickel was in fact a Soviet spy device.

With Hayhanen's help, the FBI was also finally able to decipher the message in the microdot. Strangely enough, it turned out to be a message from the KGB in Moscow to *Hayhanen*, congratulating him on his arrival in the United States and giving him instructions for his spy work! How amazing that the message had found its way to Hayhanen through such an odd chain of events!

The only mystery still to be solved was who was responsible for the nickel and its message in the first place. The FBI decided to start with the person who had acted as Hayhanen's handler while he was in the United States. Hayhanen only knew him as "Mark," although he was supposed to be a KGB colonel who had worked in **espionage** since 1927. Hayhanen also remembered that Mark was an accomplished photographer and artist. Mark had once taken Hayhanen to his apartment—something Mark never should have done, as it's not a safe practice for a spy to have such direct, personal knowledge about his handler. This error in **tradecraft** would lead to Mark's eventual arrest.

Abel's cuff link concealments.

After being driven around Brooklyn for weeks with the FBI, Hayhanen recognized Mark's apartment building and led officials to the photo studio where Mark worked. The name on the mailbox was "Emil Goldfus."

The studio was immediately put under **surveillance**. Within a week, the FBI arrested "Mark." When they searched his photo studio and the hotel room that he occupied, they found a virtual museum of modern spy equipment— short-wave radios, cipher pads, cameras, film for producing microdots, a hollow shaving brush, hollow cuff links, and numerous other concealments. They also learned that "Mark"/ "Emil Goldfus" was Rudolf Abel, a Soviet spy.

Abel was tried, found guilty, and put in prison in the U.S. But on February 10, 1962, he was exchanged for an American pilot named Francis Gary Powers, who was imprisoned after being shot down while flying a U-2 spy plane over the Soviet Union.

Upon returning to Moscow, Abel was treated as a hero, but internally the KGB blamed his arrest on a failure to follow instructions. After Hayhanen's defection in May 1957, Moscow had ordered Abel to immediately leave the United States. Had he done so, he would have avoided arrest.

Years later it was learned that even after he was caught, Abel had still fooled the FBI. By

stating his name as "Rudolf Abel" at the time of his arrest, he was sending a coded message to the KGB that he had not revealed all of their secrets. He kept his *real* name, Vilyam Fisher, hidden the whole time he was held as a prisoner, proving that he truly was a master of concealment!

Rudolf Abel (really Vilyam Fisher) creating concealments in his New York studio.

catch you later!

So, how did you *find* your training in hiding and seeking this month? Did you have fun? Hope so!

As you continue your spy training, it's a good idea to practice the new skills you gained in this month's guide. You've got the tools and the know-how to stash the most secret of secrets just about anywhere—in your room, outside, at school, or even on yourself. And you've got some great techniques for *finding* secrets, too.

But before you slip this guide into one of your new hiding places, here's a final challenge. It's a message in math code (from **Operation Number Cruncher** on page 42). Can you decode it?

$$4.15 + 14.20 \qquad 8.09 + 4.05 \qquad 25.15 + 21.18$$

$$16.18 + 9.04 \qquad 5.09 + 14.01 \qquad 10.15 + 2.23$$

$$5.12 + 12.04 \qquad 15.14 + 5.00$$

Check your answer below, and look forward to *finding* more spy secrets in your mailbox next month!

Page 42 (Spy Quest):
Look in the ugly slipper.

Page 48 (Catch You Later!):
Don't hide your pride in a job well done!

Page 44 (Operation Number Cruncher):
Secret meeting after school.

Page 44 (Operation Number Cruncher):
You can count on me.